EVERYTHING REPTILES

NATIONAL GEOGRAPHIC KiDS

D0947671

EVERYTHING REPTILES

BLAKE HOENA
With National Geographic Explorer BRADY BARR

NATIONAL GEOGRAPHIC
WASHINGTON, D.C.

CONTENTS

Green sea turtles are named for the greenish color of the cartilage and fat under their shells. These long-distance swimmers are an endangered species.

The green basilisk, or plumed basilisk lizard, is native to Central America. It can use its splayed feet to run across the surface of water for short distances.

INTRODUCTION

REPTILES ARE AMAZING
ANIMALS. THEY ARE EXTRAORDINARILY

diverse, with more than 8,000 species living almost everywhere in the world, except Antarctica. Reptiles have been around since before the dinosaurs, and they have had millions of years of experience at surviving and adapting to an ever-changing world. They were considered the most dominant animals more than 300 million years ago. Some, such as monitor lizards and crocodiles, even look as though they are from prehistoric times. Reptiles are still vital to the health of our planet today. Most are stealthy predators that help control the number of pests in a habitat. They are incredibly hardy survivors that live all around us.

Reptiles are some of the world's most remarkable, fierce, and awesomely odd creatures. Read on to learn EVERYTHING you need to know about our planet's mighty and magnificent reptiles.

EXPLORER'S CORNER

Hi! I'm Brady Barr.

I'm a herpetologist—a scientist who studies reptiles and amphibians. Crocs are my specialty. They're my favorite animals, and what I spend most of my time working on. I'm the only scientist who has ever captured and studied in the wild every species of crocodilian: alligators, crocodiles, caiman, and the gharial. It can be dangerous work, and I've had a lot of bumps and bruises to prove it. Boy, is it fun to work with some of the largest predators on the planet! I'll share some of my adventures with you throughout the book in these Explorer's Corners.

1

REPTILES REVEALED

An alligator rests with its snout above the water in the Florida Everglades. The Everglades is a vast area of wetlands in southern Florida, U.S.A., that is home to an estimated 200,000 alligators.

WHAT IS A REPTILE?

GRAN CANARIA SKINK (CARNIVORE)

REPTILES ARE SCALY CRITTERS

THAT CREEP, CRAWL, AND SLITHER. BUT THERE'S MORE TO THEM
than just scales. Birds also have scales (just check out a bird's legs!), but that doesn't make them reptiles. So what does? All reptiles have backbones, and they are considered "cold-blooded," or ectothermic. They also breathe through lungs. Even though some reptiles, such as alligators, like to lurk underwater, they still need to come up for a breath of fresh air. Reptiles are incredibly diverse. No other animals have such varied traits.

MEAT AND VEGETABLES

All crocodiles and snakes are carnivores. They prey on other animals. But many turtles, such as the painted turtle, and many lizards, such as the whiptail, are omnivores. They like to mix things up by eating some greens with their bugs and snails. Only a few reptiles, such as iguanas and tortoises, are herbivores. These vegetarians eat a strict diet of plants.

FUN IN THE SUN

You've probably heard that reptiles are cold-blooded. That doesn't mean their blood is cold, though. If you see a lizard or turtle lounging around and soaking up some rays, it's not trying to get a tan. It's simply using the sun and the environment, such as warm rocks, to warm up because it can't do it itself. A reptile's surroundings affect its body temperature. So if it's cold outside, reptiles are cold. When reptiles are cold, their entire bodies—inside and out—are chilled. It can be hard for them to get moving with cold, stiff muscles, especially after a cool night.

Reptiles use the sun to warm their bodies.

YELLOW-BLOTCHED MAP TURTLES (OMNIVORE)

A golden tree snake feasts on a tokay gecko.

GOLDEN TREE SNAKE (CARNIVORE)

REPTILE RAP THE NAME "TUATARA" MEANS "PEAKS ON THE BACK" IN NEW ZEALAND'S MAORI LANGUAGE.

DRY SKIN

People often mistakenly think of reptiles as slimy, when the real slimesters are amphibians. Scales are what make the difference. Unlike reptiles, amphibians don't have them—just compare salamanders (amphibians) and iguanas (reptiles). They may look alike, with four legs and a tail. But a salamander has a special skin that is always moist, in or out of water, whereas a lizard's scaly skin is dry.

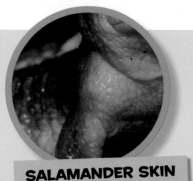

SALAMANDER SKIN

IGUANA SKIN

WHAT ISN'T A REPTILE?

Amphibians, such as salamanders, frogs, toads, and newts, are sometimes mistaken for reptiles. They are often grouped with reptiles because both are ectothermic. But amphibians and reptiles have major differences in skin, scales, and how each lives. Amphibians live mostly in and around water, which keeps their skin moist. Some also have both gills *and* lungs, whereas reptiles have only lungs. Amphibians also lay soft-shelled eggs, and their young metamorphose, or mature into adult forms. Most reptiles (except those who give birth to live young) lay hard-shelled eggs, and their young are smaller versions of the adults.

SALAMANDER

THE CLASS OF REPTILIA

The Reptilia class of animals (aka reptiles) is divided into four main orders, or groups. The largest, Squamata, includes all snakes and lizards. Then comes Testudines, which is made up of turtles and tortoises. Because of its name, it's not hard to guess that crocodiles, alligators, and caimans are part of the Crocodylia group. Lastly comes Rhynchocephalia, a special group made up of the only two living species of tuataras, which may look like iguanas but are completely different.

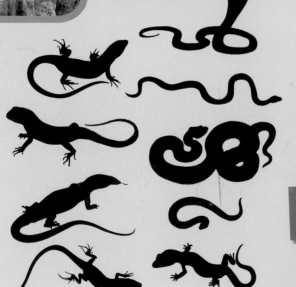

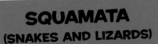

IGUANA (HERBIVORE)

SQUAMATA (SNAKES AND LIZARDS)

TESTUDINES (TURTLES AND TORTOISES)

CROCODYLIA (CAIMANS, CROCODILES, AND ALLIGATORS)

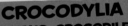

RHYNCHOCEPHALIA (TUATARAS)

SQUAMATA SQUAD

LIZARDS AND SNAKES ARE
BY FAR THE LARGEST GROUP OF REPTILES.

There are thousands and thousands of them. But snakes have no legs and most lizards have four, so why are these reptiles lumped together in the same group? They are from the Squamata order of scaled reptiles. One thing they have in common: They shed their skin, either all at once or in large strips, because they have overlapping scales. But, more importantly, it's about how their jaws are hinged. They aren't rigidly connected like human jaws. They're flexible, giving this group of reptiles the ability to open their mouth wide enough to eat large prey. Snakes and lizards also don't really chew their food but tend to swallow it whole.

Can you see the difference? A snake's eyes are always open because they have no eyelids. Lizard eyes are lidded.

SNAKE

LIZARD

SNAKES VS. LIZARDS

It's obvious how snakes are different from lizards. Snakes don't have legs, and lizards do, right? Well, believe it or not, there are some lizards, such as the slow worm, that do not have legs! So there must be other important differences. For one thing, snakes don't have visible ear openings like lizards do. They hear by sensing vibrations in the ground. Also, don't expect a snake to wink at you. Lizards have eyelids, whereas snakes cannot close their eyes. And there is one big difference that you can't see: Lizards have two full-size lungs, whereas in snakes, only the right lung is fully working. The left lung is much smaller, and in many snake species it doesn't work at all.

A green anole lizard shedding its skin

REPTILE RAP THERE ARE 9,000 SQUAMATA SPECIES.

SQUEEZERS AND BITERS

There are 18 different snake families, but most snakes fall into one of two main categories when it comes to catching and killing prey. Constrictors, such as boas and pythons, have thick, strong bodies. They bite their prey with short teeth that curve backward and are good for gripping. Once one of these snakes gets a hold of its next meal, it then starts to coil its powerful body around its prey. When its prey exhales, the snake constricts its body. It is believed that the snake does this so the animal suffocates when it can't inhale air. But some researchers say the prey dies when its blood flow is squeezed and its heart stops. When its prey is squeezed to death, the snake then eats it whole. Other snakes rely on venom to kill or paralyze their prey. How can you tell squeezers and biters apart? The biters tend to be thinner. Also, the teeth are a dead giveaway. Biters have a pair of long hollow or grooved fangs. These teeth connect to venom sacs, and when the snakes bite, venom flows through their teeth and into their prey.

BOA CONSTRICTOR

Boas are heavy snakes that use their weight to subdue prey.

With its mouth unhinged and its fangs showing, this green mamba is ready to bite.

SLOW WORMS ARE LIZARDS THAT BURROW. ALSO CALLED BLINDWORMS, THEY CAN LIVE ABOUT 30 TO 50 YEARS IN THE WILD.

SLOW WORM

TERRIFIC TESTUDINES & COOL CROCODILIANS

ANIMALS IN THE CROCODYLIA AND TESTUDINE
FAMILIES LOOK LIKE MONSTERS LEFTOVER FROM PREHISTORIC TIMES. IT'S TRUE,
crocodilians have lurked in swamps and marshes since before the dinosaurs roamed Earth. And prehistoric turtles trekked both land and sea. Actually, dinosaurs, turtles, and crocodiles are all closely related.

HOME ON YOUR BACK
The feature that sets turtles apart from all other reptiles is their carapace, or shell. They basically carry their home around on their back, as their shell provides them with protection from predators and the environment. A turtle's shell is made of scutes, or thick bony plates. Unlike snake and lizard scales, turtle scutes do not overlap, but rather interlock somewhat like building blocks. The shell also forms a turtle's rib cage and spine.

THREE OF A KIND
Testudines can be split into three categories, partly based on their habitat. Turtles, such as the loggerhead sea turtle, have flippers for motoring around in the water, where they spend most of their time. Tortoises are land reptiles and have adapted to living in deserts as well as rain forests. Then there is a nonofficial group called terrapins. These turtles are equally at home in the water and on land. They have webbed feet and often sun themselves on logs in swamps or on rocks near shore.

GREEN SEA TURTLE (TURTLE)

RED-EARED SLIDER (TERRAPIN)

RADIATED TORTOISE (TORTOISE)

The gharial is a critically endangered animal, with only 235 left in India and Nepal.

WHAT ARE GHARIALS?

Most people are familiar with crocs and gators, and even caimans, which are small gators. But what are gharials? They are a very rare crocodilian. Gharials are so rare that just over 200 remain, mostly in India. They have long, thin jaws, perfect for catching fish, their meal of choice. Males have a bulbous growth on the end of their snouts. This growth is hollow, and males use it to serenade females.

LET'S GET NOSY

Want a quick way to tell alligators and crocodiles apart? It's all in the nose. Gators and caimans have a U-shaped, rounded nose. A croc's nose is more pointed, like a V.

Another easy-to-see difference is in their toothy grins. An alligator's upper jaw is wider than its lower jaw, so when it closes its mouth, you only see some of its teeth. But this isn't true for a crocodile. When it closes its mouth, its teeth (top and bottom) jut out.

ALLIGATOR

CROCODILE

REPTILE RAP: A TURTLE'S SHELL GROWS AS ITS SMALLER SCUTES ARE SHED, ONE AT A TIME, AND REPLACED BY LARGER ONES.

REPTILE WORLD

BEING COLD-BLOODED LIMITS

WHERE REPTILES CAN LIVE, BUT THEY ARE

found in deserts, rain forests, mountains, grasslands, and even the open ocean. While most prefer warm climates, they have adapted to living in all but the coldest regions, so there is hardly a place on Earth without lizards scurrying about or snakes slithering across the ground. Turtles find homes in backyard ponds and vast oceans, and alligators and crocodiles lurk in marshes and along coasts.

GILA MONSTER

EXPLORER'S CORNER

I have worked with reptiles all over the planet, traveling to more than 80 countries for my research. My favorite part of the planet is Asia. I like to call it "the land of the giants." Asia is where you can find the world's largest crocodile, the largest lizard, the longest snake, and the largest of all sea turtles.

LEATHERBACK SEA TURTLE

NORTH AMERICA

GILA MONSTER

Living in the deserts of the southwestern United States and northern Mexico, the slow-moving Gila monster is a venomous lizard. While human fatalities are rare, the lizard's paralyzing venom and powerful jaws inflict horribly painful bites.

OPEN OCEANS

LEATHERBACK SEA TURTLE

Swimming the temperate oceans of the world, from near Alaska, U.S.A., to along Africa's southernmost tip, leatherbacks are the world's largest turtles, tipping the scales at more than 1,000 pounds (454 kg). They are also unique in having a shell made of hard leathery skin instead of a bony shell.

LEATHERBACK SEA TURTLE

NORTH AMERICA

GILA MONSTER

GREEN ANACONDA

GREEN ANACONDA

SOUTH AMERICA

GREEN ANACONDA

Among snake species, green anacondas are the heavyweights. They have been known to top 500 pounds (227 kg) and are second in length only to the reticulated python.

REPTILE RAP: LEATHERBACKS HAVE THE LONGEST MIGRATION OF ALL SEA TURTLES AT 3,000 MILES (4,828 KM).

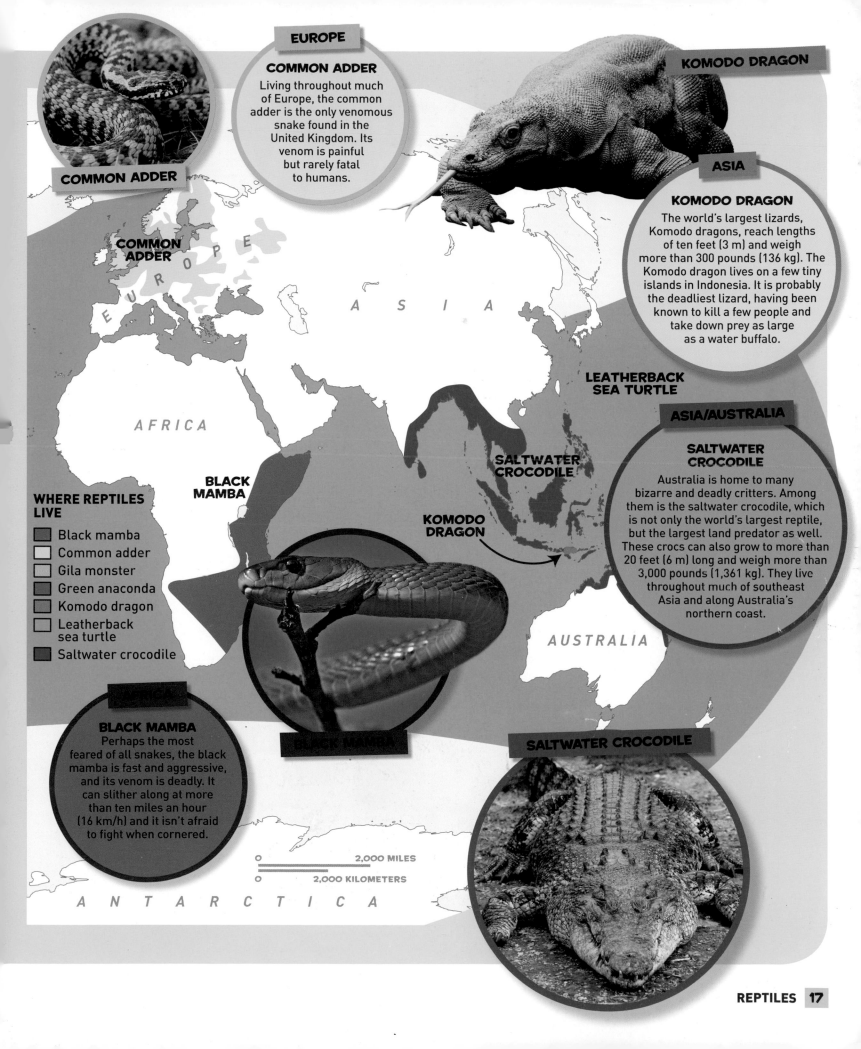

COMMON ADDER

COMMON ADDER

COMMON ADDER

EUROPE

COMMON ADDER

Living throughout much of Europe, the common adder is the only venomous snake found in the United Kingdom. Its venom is painful but rarely fatal to humans.

KOMODO DRAGON

E U R O P E

A S I A

AFRICA

ASIA

KOMODO DRAGON

The world's largest lizards, Komodo dragons, reach lengths of ten feet (3 m) and weigh more than 300 pounds (136 kg). The Komodo dragon lives on a few tiny islands in Indonesia. It is probably the deadliest lizard, having been known to kill a few people and take down prey as large as a water buffalo.

LEATHERBACK SEA TURTLE

ASIA/AUSTRALIA

SALTWATER CROCODILE

Australia is home to many bizarre and deadly critters. Among them is the saltwater crocodile, which is not only the world's largest reptile, but the largest land predator as well. These crocs can also grow to more than 20 feet (6 m) long and weigh more than 3,000 pounds (1,361 kg). They live throughout much of southeast Asia and along Australia's northern coast.

SALTWATER CROCODILE

BLACK MAMBA

KOMODO DRAGON

WHERE REPTILES LIVE

- ▢ Black mamba
- ▢ Common adder
- ▢ Gila monster
- ▢ Green anaconda
- ▢ Komodo dragon
- ▢ Leatherback sea turtle
- ▢ Saltwater crocodile

AUSTRALIA

AFRICA

BLACK MAMBA

Perhaps the most feared of all snakes, the black mamba is fast and aggressive, and its venom is deadly. It can slither along at more than ten miles an hour (16 km/h) and it isn't afraid to fight when cornered.

BLACK MAMBA

SALTWATER CROCODILE

0 ━━━━━ 2,000 MILES

0 ━━━━━ 2,000 KILOMETERS

A N T A R C T I C A

A PHOTOGRAPHIC DIAGRAM

COOL CHAMELEONS

WOULDN'T IT BE COOL IF
YOU COULD CHANGE YOUR SKIN COLOR TO
send a message or suit your mood? What if you could change color to match your surroundings and blend into the background? Chameleons are expert skin-color communicators and camouflage artists. But those aren't the only awesome adaptations they have. Just take a look!

VISE GRIPS
Chameleon feet look like pincers. They are strong and great for holding on to tree branches.

WALK LIKE A CHAMELEON
Have you ever watched a chameleon walk? It may look painfully slow and hesitant, wavering back and forth as though it isn't sure of its next step. This is actually a form of camouflage. The chameleon is trying to mimic the movement of its surroundings, such as a tree branch blowing in the wind.

360-DEGREE VISION

Chameleon eyes stick out and can move independently of each other. This allows chameleons to see all around them. They can spot a snake trying to sneak up on them and a beetle trying to escape being eaten at the same time.

COLD-BLOODED

Reptiles are ectothermic, which means they do not regulate their body temperature like people do, so they do not need as much energy. That's one big advantage for survival. People eat every day, and part of that food energy goes toward keeping our body temperature at 98.6°F (37°C). But reptiles do not use energy to maintain body heat, and because of that, some can go days, weeks, and even months without eating.

SCALY SKIN

Unlike fish scales, reptile scales are actually a layer of skin. Fish scales can come off one at a time because they are attached to the skin—but not reptile scales. Their scales are all connected to each other and this is why they come off together instead of one at a time. The big benefit of their scaly skin is that it helps keep moisture in their bodies, which allows reptiles to live in very dry places.

CAMOUFLAGE, COMMUNICATE, KEEP COOL

Chameleons can change the color of their skin, which helps them hide from predators. They can even communicate with each other through their color changes, usually for mating purposes. Changing their skin color also helps regulate their body temperature. Other lizard and snake species are also able to lighten or darken their skin for this purpose.

The bush viper is a venomous snake native to Central Africa. It climbs trees and reeds and feasts on frogs, lizards, and small mammals.

2
REPTILE LIFE

LIFE CYCLE

MOST REPTILES REPRODUCE IN THE USUAL WAY. BOY REPTILE MEETS GIRL REPTILE.

Boy impresses girl, whether it's by bellowing and grunting (crocodiles), turning brilliant colors (chameleons), or showing off cool dance moves (some snakes). Months after reptiles mate, the female lays eggs, and then young reptiles hatch from those eggs. But in the diverse world of reptiles, there are a few species that do things differently.

ON THEIR OWN

Most female reptiles hide their eggs. They bury them in the ground to keep them warm and safe. Most reptiles do not stick around long enough to see if their eggs hatch. Female long-tailed skinks are one of the few reptiles that will stay to defend their eggs. And they are tough. They will take on a hungry, egg-eating snake to keep their unhatched young safe. Once the young skinks break out of their shells, they are on their own. Alligators are also protective of their eggs and young. When young gators hatch, they start to chirp, alerting their mother of their arrival. She uncovers her nest so her hatchlings can venture out into the world. For the first years of their lives, young gators stick around their mother. She will defend her babies from bigger gators that might view them as food.

Male panamint rattlesnakes dance to gain the attention of a mate.

NO FERTILIZATION REQUIRED

Whiptail lizards and dwarf tree geckos are among the lizard species that have only female members. They can reproduce through parthenogenesis, which means their eggs do not need to be fertilized by a male.

New Mexico whiptails are all female.

REPTILE RAP: ALLIGATOR MOTHERS CARRY NEW HATCHLINGS IN THEIR MOUTHS.

OVIPAROUS VS. OVOVIVIPAROUS VS. VIVIPAROUS

There's no need to bust out your dictionary, these words are simple to understand, although hard to pronounce.

- **OVIPAROUS** means a female animal lays eggs, and then young eventually hatch from those eggs. Birds are oviparous, and so are most reptiles, such as alligators and turtles.
Advantage: Oviparous animals can lay large clutches of eggs at a time.

- **OVOVIVIPAROUS** means a female produces eggs, but those eggs stay within her body to develop. When the eggs hatch, the female gives birth to live young. Many sharks are ovoviviparous, and so are some reptiles, such as eyelash vipers and short-horned lizards.
Advantage: The young of ovoviviparous animals tend to be more fully functioning at birth than oviparous young.

- **VIVIPAROUS** means that a female gives birth to live young. Humans and almost all other mammals are viviparous, along with a few reptiles, such as tussock skinks and the *Mabuya* genus of skinks.
Advantage: Young developing inside their mother are better protected from predators and the elements than eggs buried in a hole in the ground.

EYELASH VIPER
(OVOVIVIPAROUS)

ALLIGATORS
(OVIPAROUS)

SOUTHERN GRASS
TUSSOCK SKINK
(VIVIPAROUS)

By the Numbers

10 years is the average life span for chameleons.

30 years is how long boa constrictors usually live.

50 years of roaming swamps is the average life for alligators.

80 years of life is average for sea turtles.

100 years or more is how long giant tortoises can live.

PREDATORS AND PREY

REPTILES ARE DEADLY AND ADAPTABLE HUNTERS.

THIS IS HOW THEY HAVE SURVIVED FOR MILLIONS OF YEARS. MANY REPTILES ALSO HAVE specialized diets, which is why several types of reptiles can live in the same area. They don't all eat the same thing. While one lizard, such as a green iguana, may prefer a diet of greens, another kind of lizard might chomp on insects. Some, such as monitor lizards, will even munch on snakes. That means different types of lizards can happily be neighbors without fighting over their next meal. This is also true among snakes. Some will dig up a lizard's eggs and others will hunt for adults. Having such varied diets between animals is one reason there are so many reptile species. If they aren't competing for the same food, more kinds can survive.

IT THAT A LOG?

The camouflage coloring of some prey animals allows them to blend in with their surroundings. But it works both ways. Predators can also use camouflage to sneak up on prey. Crocodiles and alligators have dark, scaly backs. In murky swamp water, they are often mistaken for floating logs. To help them with their disguise, their nostrils are on the top of their snouts, and their eyes are on the top of their heads. They can see and breathe easily, while only a small portion of their bodies are visible. Alligators and crocodiles lurk near the surface of the water, slowly moving toward prey. They must be quick and agile to take prey by surprise.

Crocodiles use their tails to propel through water. They rest a lot but can have explosive bursts of speed in water and on land. They may drag their prey underwater to kill it, but they eat on land or with their heads above the water.

REPTILE RAP: SALTWATER CROCODILES ARE BELIEVED TO HAVE THE STRONGEST BITE OF ANY ANIMAL.

MORE THAN A MOUTHFUL

The green anaconda is a mighty constrictor snake known to tangle with caimans and swallow them whole. The snake's hinged jaw allows it to open its mouth extra wide and tackle meals larger than its head. Eating such large meals all at once allows an anaconda to go for months without needing to eat again.

VEGETARIAN REPTILES

Most reptiles are carnivores, or meat-eaters. A few reptiles are herbivores, or plant-eaters. Iguanas eat a strict diet of greens. But they are in the minority. A desert tortoise is one such plant-eater. Its diet is made up of wildflowers and grasses. With its hardened beak and powerful jaws, this tortoise can even snack on cacti.

VENOMOUS LIZARDS

At one time, scientists thought there were only two venomous lizards—the Gila monster and the Mexican beaded lizard. With more research, scientists determined that other reptiles have venomous bites as well. These include members of the monitor lizard and the iguana families. For the most part, lizard venom is less dangerous than snake venom. But it is still painful.

The Komodo dragon is a lizard known for its venomous bite. Komodos are machinelike hunters. They will attack animals far larger than themselves, such as water buffalo. If an animal is bitten by a Komodo dragon, the smell of blood from the wound will attract other Komodos. The venom will slowly weaken the animal as more Komodo dragons gather and follow the wounded animal. Eventually, when the bitten animal is too weak to defend itself, the Komodo dragons go in for the kill.

KOMODO DRAGON

DEADLY BITES

Snake venom is designed to paralyze and kill prey. When snakes bite, the venom flows through hollow, or grooved, fangs and into their prey. After a strike, they wait for the venom to do its work before swallowing their prey whole. Many snakes, such as rattlesnakes and vipers, have venom that is potentially deadly to humans. One of the most venomous animals in the world, and possibly the deadliest snake, is the inland taipan. One strike-size dose of its venom can kill up to 100 people. If bitten, a person could die within an hour if not treated. But luckily, most venomous snakes try to avoid larger animals—no point in attacking an animal that is too big to swallow. And even if they bite in defense, snakes don't always deliver venom. It takes a lot of energy for snakes to create venom, so they prefer to use it on food.

INLAND TAIPAN

SUPER SURVIVORS

REPTILE LIFE IS NOT JUST ABOUT HUNTING SKILLS.

THE HUNTED ALSO HAVE A FEW TRICKS TO STAY SAFE AND SURVIVE. Some, such as geckos and snakes, rely on their appearance to provide camouflage. Others, such as crocodiles and alligators, whip their powerful tails around to keep predators safely away. Survival skills are as varied as species in the reptile world.

CORAL SNAKE

MISTAKEN IDENTITY

Scarlet kingsnakes use their coloring to their advantage. Kingsnakes can easily be mistaken for venomous coral snakes, since they have similar yellow, black, and red patterned skin. Predators don't want to risk a deadly bite, so they are likely to avoid a scarlet kingsnake as though it were a coral snake. The key difference keen eyes will notice is that red touches black on the kingsnake, whereas red touches yellow on the coral snake.

SCARLET KINGSNAKE

EXPLORER'S CORNER

One of my favorite reptile defense strategies is the one used by the eastern hognose snake. When it feels threatened, it rolls onto its back, goes limp, and sticks its tongue out, playing dead. It does all of this in the hope that whatever is bothering it will lose interest in a dead animal and go on its way. Once the eastern hognose feels safe, it flips back over, puts its tongue back in its mouth, and safely slithers away!

BLUESTRIPE GARTER SNAKE

WHAT'S THAT SMELL?

Nobody, not even a hungry predator, wants to bite into something that tastes horrible. So as a defense mechanism, some reptiles will emit a foul-smelling (and tasting) substance. Cottonmouth snakes emit a stinky substance when threatened. And so do garter snakes. If you pick one up, be careful, because your hands may become covered in this nasty stuff. The snake gives this off to make you let go of it.

Hey, where's my tail? A Mediterranean gecko can drop its tail to avoid a predator.

DID YOU FORGET SOMETHING?

If a predator wants to avoid being bitten or scratched by a lizard, it's safest to grab it by the tail. But even if a lizard is caught this way by a predator, that doesn't mean it will become dinner. Tuataras and some lizards, such as geckos and skinks, have a trick for getting away under such circumstances. They will wiggle vigorously, which causes a break in their skin and muscles. The end of their tail then breaks off. To make their getaway even easier, the tail keeps wiggling after it's detached, so the predator thinks it still has a hold on its meal. A lizard without its tail will be off-balance, making it more difficult to climb and run, but it's better than being eaten. Plus, its tail will eventually grow back.

BIGGER THAN YOU!

In the reptile world, it's more common that a snake will prey on a lizard than the other way around. And in a fight, a snake often has the advantage since it either has deadly venom or a powerful body to constrict its prey. Sometimes, avoiding a fight is the better option. Despite opening their mouths wide, there is a limit to what snakes can swallow. Some lizards will use this to their advantage. When face to face with a predator, a desert horned lizard, which has a wide body, will turn on its side, making it appear too big to eat. Frilled lizards take this trick to a new level. They have a ruffled collar around their neck, which they can expand to make themselves look bigger and scarier as they stand on their hind legs.

FRILLED LIZARD

REPTILE RAP: SOME COBRAS DEFEND THEMSELVES BY SPITTING BLINDING VENOM AT PREDATORS.

HOMES AND HABITATS

MOST REPTILES PREFER WARM
WEATHER SINCE THEY ARE ECTOTHERMS—ANIMALS

that rely on their surroundings to regulate their body temperature. We commonly think of lizards and snakes as living in hot deserts or rain forests, and in fact, that's where the majority of reptiles live. But reptiles are very diverse, so there are snakes, lizards, and even turtles in all but the coldest regions of the world.

These snakes are emerging from hibernation.

A lizard rests on a rock.

DEEP SLEEP

Like some mammals, reptiles hibernate—or, more correctly, they brumate. Hibernation and brumation are the same thing. Both refer to a state of dormancy some animals enter into during the colder months when food is scarce. Brumation is the term used for reptiles. During brumation they do not move, and so they survive with very little oxygen. Turtles may sink into the mud at the bottom of a pond. Lizards will bury themselves in the dirt, and snakes crawl into an underground den. The ground they are under actually insulates the reptiles to keep them from freezing during the winter.

HOME SWEET HOME

Each reptile species has a preferred habitat. Within its habitat, it may have a favorite pile of logs or rocks to hide under, or one pond it spends its entire life in. Although they move around a lot to find food, reptiles stay put while brumating or nesting. Some den-dwelling reptiles spend the winter in the same den from year to year. Others, such as loggerhead sea turtles, roam the oceans but return to the exact beach where they hatched to lay their own clutch of eggs.

REPTILE RAP: DESERT CHAMELEONS CAN MAKE THE TOP OF THEIR BODIES LIGHT COLORED TO REFLECT THE SUN'S HEAT.

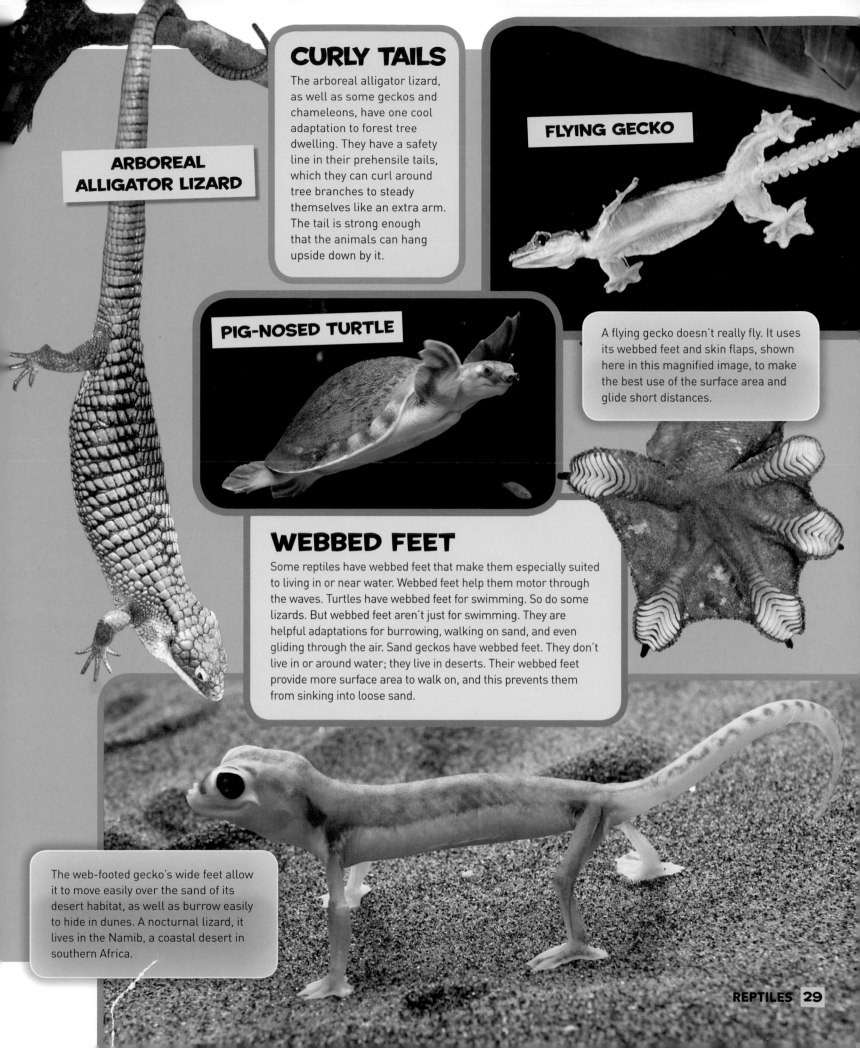

CURLY TAILS

The arboreal alligator lizard, as well as some geckos and chameleons, have one cool adaptation to forest tree dwelling. They have a safety line in their prehensile tails, which they can curl around tree branches to steady themselves like an extra arm. The tail is strong enough that the animals can hang upside down by it.

ARBOREAL ALLIGATOR LIZARD

FLYING GECKO

A flying gecko doesn't really fly. It uses its webbed feet and skin flaps, shown here in this magnified image, to make the best use of the surface area and glide short distances.

PIG-NOSED TURTLE

WEBBED FEET

Some reptiles have webbed feet that make them especially suited to living in or near water. Webbed feet help them motor through the waves. Turtles have webbed feet for swimming. So do some lizards. But webbed feet aren't just for swimming. They are helpful adaptations for burrowing, walking on sand, and even gliding through the air. Sand geckos have webbed feet. They don't live in or around water; they live in deserts. Their webbed feet provide more surface area to walk on, and this prevents them from sinking into loose sand.

The web-footed gecko's wide feet allow it to move easily over the sand of its desert habitat, as well as burrow easily to hide in dunes. A nocturnal lizard, it lives in the Namib, a coastal desert in southern Africa.

A PHOTO GALLERY

THE WORLD OF REPTILES IS FILLED WITH amazing critters, ranging in size from the width of your finger to the size of your family car. Some are colorful, and some are plain. Others just look odd, or will make you say "wow!"

WOW! REPTILES!

Some snake-necked turtles have necks so long that they cannot completely retract them into their shells.

Some spitting cobras can appear more threatening by squirting venom up to 6.6 feet (2 m) out of their glands and through their fangs.

The Gaboon viper weighs in as the world's heaviest viper at 17.6 pounds (8 kg). But it is a lightweight compared to some reticulated pythons, which can weigh up to 350 pounds (159 kg).

The blood that a horned lizard squirts from the corners of its eyes tastes nasty and keeps dog and cat predators away.

The sharp spikes of a thorny dragon, also known as a thorny devil, are meant to discourage attacks from predators.

Is that a lizard in a superhero costume? The male agama lizard's coloring turns orange, red, pink, and blue to attract a female during mating season.

It's a turtle that looks like an alligator! The alligator snapping turtle has powerful jaws and a spiny shell.

Plesiosaurs were prehistoric marine reptiles that had four flippers and a tail. Some had short necks, and some had long ones. They varied in size between 5 feet (1.5 m) and 40 feet (12 m).

RISE OF THE REPTILES

3

WHEN REPTILES RULED

JUST TAKE A LOOK AT SOME OF TODAY'S LARGEST

REPTILES, FROM CROCODILES TO MONITOR LIZARDS, PYTHONS, AND GIANT SEA turtles. It's not hard to imagine that they ruled the planet once upon a time. With their scaly skin and powerful jaws, they look like creatures from a bygone era. And they are!

FIRST CAME THE EGG

The first reptiles appeared late in the Carboniferous period (360–300 million years ago), a time when amphibians were the predominant animals on Earth. The planet was much more swamp-like then, which was perfect for large labyrinthodonts, alligator-like amphibians with sharp teeth. Some of the reptiles that lived during that time period started laying amniotic eggs, or eggs with an outer shell. At first, that shell wasn't hard like a bird egg. It was more of a thick membrane. The membrane kept the egg from drying out, so it didn't need to be in water. It also held the yolk sac, which provided the embryo with the nutrients it needed to survive and develop until the reptile hatched. Amniotic eggs allowed animals to venture farther from the water than they had in the past.

A kneeling man illustrates the size of a prehistoric and contemporary croc's jaws. Fossil specimens show SuperCroc measured as long as 40 feet (12 m).

REPTILE RAP: ARCHELON, A GIANT PREHISTORIC SEA TURTLE, WEIGHED MORE THAN 4,850 POUNDS (2,200 KG).

HYLONOMUS

THE FIRST REPTILE

Hylonomus, possibly the first reptile, was about the size of a large gecko. But it looked similar to reptiles as we know them now. It had a long tail and four legs. Its skin was scaly, and it had sharp teeth. Mostly, it scurried around forests eating insects and trying not to be eaten by large amphibians.

DIMETRODON

RISE AND FALL OF REPTILES

About 250 million years ago, at the end of the Permian period, there was a mass extinction. It is believed that more than 90 percent of all animal species died out, probably because the planet was extremely hot with a lot of volcanic activity. Reptiles were able to survive the hotter climate better than amphibians. Over time, reptiles became the predominant animals. While a heating-up period helped reptiles (and dinosaurs) grow to massive size, a cooling-down period probably caused their demise. Scientists believe that about 65 million years ago an asteroid struck Earth. Millions of tons of dust and debris were kicked up into the atmosphere, blocking out the sun's warming rays. Being mostly ectotherms, the large reptiles fared poorly in the colder weather and many died out. This allowed the more adaptable mammals, with their protective fur, to spread throughout the land.

RULERS OF THE AGES

During the Paleozoic era, also called the age of invertebrates, animals with backbones began to appear. At first, tiny trilobites became the dominant creatures, then fish, and lastly, amphibians. Other eras followed:

MESOZOIC ERA
THE AGE OF REPTILES

Large reptiles ruled the land, sea, and air.

TRIASSIC PERIOD
(250 MILLION–200 MILLION YEARS AGO):

Large reptiles, such as archosaurs, stomped around. They are the ancestors of crocodiles and dinosaurs. Toward the end of this period, turtle-like reptiles first appeared, as did the tuatara's earliest relatives.

JURASSIC PERIOD
(200 MILLION–145 MILLION YEARS AGO)

While dinosaurs first appeared in the Triassic period, this was the time they truly came to rule the land. It was also the time when members of Squamata (modern-day lizards) first scurried about.

CRETACEOUS PERIOD
(145 MILLION–65 MILLION YEARS AGO)

Some of the first snakes are believed to have lost their legs during this period. It is also the time when theropods, such as *T. rex* and *Spinosaurus*, were the largest land predators.

CENOZOIC ERA
THE AGE OF MAMMALS

The end of the Mesozoic era saw the extinction of all dinosaurs, except birds, and many other large reptiles. This allowed the highly adaptable mammals to become the dominant animals.

SUPERCROC AND FLYING REPTILES

Sarcosuchus is an extinct distant relative of modern crocodiles.

MODERN-DAY REPTILES
WOULD BE HARD-PRESSED TO COMPETE

with the size and ferocity of some of their prehistoric cousins. Hungry snapping crocodiles are intimidating enough, but imagine coming face-to-face with a SuperCroc or a massive flying pterosaur!

SUPERCROC

Saltwater crocodiles are not only the largest reptiles today, they are also the largest land predators. But do you think they could take on dinosaurs? Sarcosuchus could. These crocodile-like beasts roamed the land around 110 million years ago, measured 40 feet (12 m) long, and tipped the scales at about 9 tons (8.2 MT). Add to that foot-long (0.3-m) teeth and incredibly powerful jaws, and you have a SuperCroc, one that could defend its territory from even the mighty Spinosaurus. The remains of Sarcosuchus were found in northern Africa, in a desert. Millions of years ago, this area wasn't covered in sand. It was swampland filled with fish, Sarcosuchus's favorite meal.

REPTILE RAP: SARCOSUCHUS WASN'T A CROCODILE, BUT A RELATIVE OF A CROCODILE-LIKE REPTILE CALLED PHOLIDOSAURUS.

SUPERSNAKE

It seems as though everything in prehistoric times came supersized, and that was also true of snakes. Fossils of what scientists believe was a 40-foot (12-m)-long snake that weighed about a ton (0.9 MT), were found in South America. *Titanoboa* lived about 60 million years ago. The amazing thing about this find is that researchers found a skull. Snake skulls are made of delicate bones and tend to just fall apart over time. But *Titanoboa* was buried in a mudslide, which helped preserve it.

TITANOBOA

DEINOSUCHUS

SUPERGATOR

While Africa had its SuperCroc, North America had *Deinosuchus.* It was probably smaller than *Sarcosuchus,* though still more than 30 feet (9 m) long. It lived about 80 million years ago and mostly ate fish. But some dinosaur remains show teeth marks from *Deinosuchus's* bite, which means it may have chomped on small dinos, too.

By the Numbers

40 feet (12 m) is the estimated length of a *Sarcosuchus.*

30 feet (9 m) of snapping jaws and a powerful tail made *Deinosuchus* a ferocious and now extinct relative of the alligator.

23 feet (7 m) from nose to tail, the saltwater crocodile is the largest living crocodilian.

15 feet (4.6 m) is how long an average American alligator measures.

PTERODACTYLUS

FLYING REPTILES

Before there were birds, pterosaurs soared overhead. These reptiles were the first vertebrates (animals with backbones) to fly, with the largest having nearly a 40-foot (12-m) wingspan. They lived during the time of dinosaurs, but do not mistake them for dinos. And while they had hollow bones like birds, they weren't ancient birds, either. Modern reptiles do not fly like pterosaurs, but some lizards and geckos can glide. The draco lizard has specialized ribs with attached skin flaps that it can extend to glide. Asian flying geckos also use skin flaps on the side of their heads and necks to help them parachute from tree to tree.

REPTILE RESEARCH

SOME REPTILES ARE LIVING

FOSSILS. THEY HAVE NOT CHANGED MUCH OVER millions and millions of years. Their ability to survive when so many other animals have become extinct is amazing, and it is one very important reason to study them. Through learning more about reptiles, scientists can understand the effects our ever-changing world has on animals, the environment, and us.

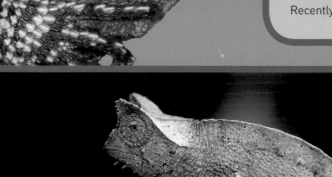

DWARF DRAGON

UNEARTHING NEW REPTILES

While paleontologists are continually discovering and digging up the bones, or fossils, of extinct prehistoric animals, herpetologists continue to uncover new, never before seen living reptiles. Remote rain forests tend to be the best places for these undiscovered critters to hide. Several new species of wood lizards, commonly called dwarf dragons because of their spiky backs, were discovered along the border of Ecuador and Peru. The island of Madagascar, off the coast of Africa, is another hotbed of new discoveries. Recently, a nocturnal gecko species was discovered, as well as the tiny leaf chameleon.

LEAF CHAMELEON

LIVING FOSSILS

Scientists actually consider tuataras to be living fossils. Their closest relatives in the reptile world died out around the same time as the dinosaurs. It is believed that these lizard-like reptiles have not changed over millions of years. They walk more like frogs than lizards and have simple, single-chamber hearts. Studying them teaches scientists what more primitive life was like millions of years ago.

REPTILE RAP: RATS ARE A MAJOR THREAT TO THE SURVIVAL OF WILD TUATARA.

PARIETAL EYE

FOREHEAD EYE

One of the oddest features of the tuatara is its third eye on the top of its head. It has the basic parts of a normal eye, but scientists do not believe it is for seeing. The eye is sensitive to light. Called a parietal eye, the feature is also common in many squamates, or scaled reptiles. But for them, the eye is more of an opening in the skull covered by scaly skin. It is believed that this eye helps reptiles judge seasonal changes in daylight.

NOCTURNAL GECKO

The nocturnal gecko was only discovered by researchers in 2004.

ENDANGERED ANIMALS

Every year, a handful of reptile species becomes extinct. And experts believe that nearly 20 percent of all reptiles are in some danger of dying out. Human activity can change reptile habitats in harmful ways. Many species of reptiles are very specialized, meaning they cannot adapt well to changes in their diets or how they live. Some, such as the newly discovered nocturnal gecko in Madagascar, have a habitat of less than 20 square miles (52 sq km). Small environmental changes, whether caused by pollution, deforestation, or rising temperatures, can affect such a small area. These changes can kill off a species or greatly reduce its numbers.

TUATARA

Found only on New Zealand's 32 offshore islands, tuataras are the only surviving members of the Sphenodontia order.

EXPLORER'S CORNER

Crocs have been on the planet since the time of the dinosaurs. That's roughly 226 million years. Today, a third of all croc species are endangered, or threatened with extinction. This is mostly due to the actions of humans. Humans kill them out of fear or ignorance. They also destroy their habitat through logging or farming. Poachers use illegal fishing and hunting techniques in their quest for bush meat. In the bush-meat trade, crocs are poached and sold for food. This is a great threat to croc populations. Conservation efforts are helping to preserve as many crocs as possible for the future.

AMAZING JOURNEY

Sea turtles are ancient animals that have survived as a species for hundreds of millions of years.

REPTILES DON'T
OFTEN VENTURE FAR, WHICH is partially based on being adapted to their habitat, but also because many have certain foods they prefer, and they like to stick around their food sources. But the ones that do travel make some awesome journeys in time and distance.

SUPER SWIMMERS

Sea turtles have soft, leathery shells that are lighter than similar-size hard shells. They are also more aerodynamic. This helps make these turtles excellent swimmers. They spend their lives in the ocean, and some journey 10,000 miles (16,093 km) in a year. Why all the traveling? Like many migrating animals, they move in search of food. As one area of the oceans cools and another warms, their food moves, and so they follow.

NESTING GROUNDS

Leatherback sea turtles migrate for a very important reason: to come ashore and lay their eggs. Each year, they return to lay their eggs in the same nesting grounds where they hatched. Nesting sites are in Central America and the northern coast of South America. During the nesting season, female leatherbacks come ashore and dig a shallow nest in the sand to lay a clutch of eggs, which they bury. They then head back into the sea. A single leatherback will come ashore several times during the nesting season and lay about 80 eggs. About two months later, the eggs hatch. The hatchlings dig out of their sandy nest, and make a mad dash across the beach to the ocean, where they will spend much of their lives. Other sea turtle species make similar nesting journeys.

LEATHERBACK SEA TURTLE

SPERM WHALE

DEEP-SEA DIVERS

Whales are the only air-breathing animals that could beat a sea turtle in a diving contest. Leatherbacks can dive to depths of 4,200 feet (1,280 m) and stay underwater for about an hour and a half. Sperm whales can dive even deeper—down to 7,382 feet (2,250 m)—for the same amount of time.

FOR SHE'S A JOLLY OLD FELLOW

Turtles and tortoises are long-lived animals. Leatherback sea turtles are believed to have life spans similar to or longer than a human's. It's hard to celebrate birthdays for animals in the wild, but that's not true of Harriet the giant Galápagos land tortoise. She was found by naturalist Charles Darwin in 1835, when she was probably only a few years old. Harriet eventually made her way to the Australia Zoo, where she passed away in 2006. That made her more than 170 years old.

TURTLE EXTINCTION?

There are seven species of sea turtles, and sadly they are all in danger of extinction. They range from vulnerable (at risk from habitat loss) to critically endangered (at high risk of extinction). Threats to sea turtles mostly come from people, as the turtles are caught for food or accidentally get entangled and die in fishing nets. Coastal development also affects sea turtle populations, since some of their nesting grounds have been taken over by the development of beachfront property.

HAWKSBILL
CRITICALLY ENDANGERED

LEATHERBACK
CRITICALLY ENDANGERED

KEMP'S RIDLEY
CRITICALLY ENDANGERED

LOGGERHEAD
ENDANGERED

GREEN
SEA TURTLE
ENDANGERED

OLIVE RIDLEY
VULNERABLE

FLATBACK
STATUS UNKNOWN

REPTILE RAP: SEA TURTLES CAN SLEEP WHILE FLOATING ON THE OCEAN SURFACE.

REPTILE COMPARISONS

YOU VS. REPTILES

HUMANS HAVE NOT BEEN AROUND NEARLY AS LONG

as reptiles. While we can use tools and outsmart them with our bigger brains, reptiles have had hundreds of millions of years to adapt with some astounding abilities and weird (to us) traits. See how you compare to the world's amazing reptiles.

RUNNING ACROSS WATER

Green basilisk lizards are known for quick escapes. Their legs pump so fast that, with their webbed feet, they can sprint across the surface of the water. To achieve the same feat, you would need to run about 100 miles an hour (161 km/h) while wearing a pair of flippers.

MORE THAN A MOUTHFUL

Snakes can open their jaws very wide. So wide, in fact, that their meals can be wider than their midsections. That would be similar to you swallowing a soccer ball whole.

TONGUE FOR A SNIFFER

For the most part, humans and reptiles have similar senses, although we may see, hear, and feel things a little differently. The big difference comes with the senses of smell and taste. For reptiles, these senses are combined. When reptiles, especially snakes, stick out their tongues, they are catching scent particles in the air. They are smelling with their tongues. As humans, we inhale scents through our noses.

KNIGHTS IN SCALY ARMOR

Once upon a time, people wore suits of armor during battles. Imagine that you, like a turtle, could never get out of that armor. Depending on the armor (soft shell or hard shell) and how big you are, you could be carrying around an extra 5 to 30 pounds (2.3 to 13.6 kg).

COSTUMED CRUSADERS

People come in all shapes, sizes, and colors, but that's nothing compared to the variety of reptiles. They can be all colors of the rainbow, from dull brown desert lizards to brilliantly colored agama lizards. You would need to dress up in a superhero costume to compete.

Ah, that feels good! Turtles bask in the sun to strengthen their shells. They absorb vitamin D from the sun, which helps their bony shells form properly.

4

FUN WITH REPTILES

AMAZING REPTILE FEATS!

REPTILES ARE AMAZING IN

MANY WAYS. SOMETIMES FRIGHTENING, SOMETIMES awesome. Let's check out the weird, scary, and incredible things that reptiles are known for.

DANCING LIZARDS!

Have you ever walked across the beach on a sunny day? The sand can get hot—too hot to walk on. Imagine what lizards have to deal with in the desert. Some desert lizards have taken up a dancing-like motion. They lift one back foot and the opposite foot into the air to cool them off. Then they switch feet, going back and forth as though doing a two-step.

TONGUE SLINGER

A chameleon's tongue can be as long as or longer than its body, from nose to tail. And it's fast—shooting out to its full length in a fraction of a second. It also has a sticky, glue-like tip that doesn't let go once it strikes a bug. Top that off with eyes that can rotate in two directions at the same time to help a chameleon pinpoint its prey's exact location with killer aim.

REPTILE RAP: GABOON VIPERS HAVE THE LONGEST FANGS OF ANY SNAKE, AT TWO INCHES (5 CM) LONG.

JAWS OF STEEL

When crocodiles and alligators clamp down on something, they exert thousands of pounds of pressure on whatever critter they are chomping. Their bite is literally bone crushing. Scientists who study crocs and gators don't want that force coming down on their hands. So they clamp or tape their subjects' mouths shut while working with them. This temporary clamp does not hurt the animals.

MOST DEATHS BY BITE

The Russell's viper is known for its aggressiveness. It lives in grassy areas and near rice paddies in Asia. Its bites cause more deaths than those of any other venomous snake. The viper's diluted venom is used in medical tests because it is so effective in clotting blood.

Milking the venom of a Russell's viper into a cup of blood will make the blood form into clots.

REPTILE MATCH

Reptiles and their behaviors have slithered their way into the English language for centuries. Phrases that mention reptiles can have positive or negative meanings. Can you match the phrase to its definition?

1 SNAKE OIL

2 SNAKE IN THE GRASS

3 SLOW AS A TORTOISE

4 SPEAKING WITH A FORKED TONGUE

5 TURN TURTLE

6 COME OUT OF ONE'S SHELL

7 SNAKE EYES

8 CROCODILE TEARS

A TO SHOW SADNESS BUT NOT REALLY MEAN IT

B SOMEONE WHO STOPS BEING SHY

C A MEDICINE THAT DOESN'T WORK

D SAYING ONE THING BUT DOING SOMETHING TOTALLY DIFFERENT

E SOMEONE WHO IS SNEAKY

F SOMEONE WHO DOESN'T MOVE FAST

G TO FLIP SOMETHING UPSIDE DOWN

H TWO DICE THAT ARE SHOWING ONES

ANSWERS: 1. C; 2. E; 3. F; 4. D; 5. G; 6. B; 7. H; 8. A

SPOT THE DIFFERENCE

HAVE YOU EVER MISTAKEN
A PERSON FOR SOMEBODY ELSE? WHAT WAS it that made you think the two were alike? Was it the shape of their face or the color of their hair? To the observant eye, all reptiles have revealing traits that help us tell them apart. How keen is your sight? Can you tell these reptiles apart?

BOA OR VIPER

Some snakes have brightly colored scales to try to fool predators into thinking they're venomous. But one key feature to look for is the shape of a snake's head. Venomous snakes have wide, triangular heads (to provide room for their venom sacks) that are much broader than their necks. Nonvenomous snakes have longer, narrower heads.

1. WHICH IS WHICH?
RAINBOW BOA vs. BUSH VIPER

LIZARD OR TUATARA

If you're anywhere but in New Zealand, you're looking at a lizard. But the key external difference to look for is that lizards have ear openings and tuataras don't.

2. WHO IS WHO?
TUATARA vs. GREEN IGUANA

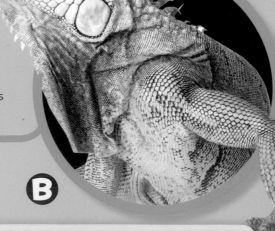

REPTILE RAP: GODZILLA IS PROBABLY THE MOST FAMOUS MOVIE REPTILE, HAVING STARRED IN ABOUT 30 MOVIES.

ANSWERS: 1. A. Bush viper, B. Rainbow boa; **2.** A. Tuatara, B. Green iguana; **3.** A. Aesculapian snake, B European worm lizard; **4.** A. African spurred tortoise, B. Red-eared slider.

SNAKE OR WORM LIZARD

Snakes aren't the only reptiles to go legless. There are nearly 180 species in the worm lizard family. For starters, worm lizards aren't always 100 percent without legs. They might have short, stubby, nearly useless legs, or bumps on their bodies where legs would have been. Snakes also don't have ear holes or eyelids, but worm lizards do. Snakes have thin tongues, while worm lizards have thick tongues. Also, worm lizards don't have wide scales on their bellies, but snakes do.

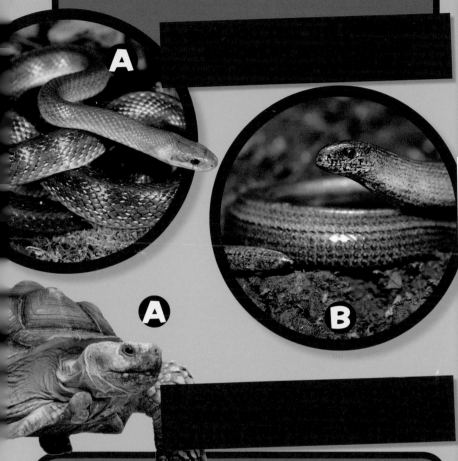

A

A

B

TURTLE OR TORTOISE

Many people think that turtles and tortoises are the same, but there are big differences between them. For starters, turtles live a large part of their lives in water, whereas tortoises are land dwellers. Turtles have webbed feet—some even look more like flippers than feet. Tortoises have stubby, rounded feet to walk on. Turtle and tortoise shells are also designed differently. Turtle shells are flatter, so they offer less resistance when turtles swim through the water. Tortoises have dome-shaped shells.

B

REPTILES IN THE MOVIES

Have you ever seen a movie like *Lassie* or *Babe* with reptile stars? If you said no, it's not surprising. Reptiles are most often portrayed in movies as the monsters people run from. But no real-life snake, crocodilian, or lizard can match the sheer size or ferocity of these movie terrors.

ANACONDA, 1997

In the Amazon, a 40-foot (12.2-m) anaconda attacks a film crew. Several spinoff movies were made with the same killer-snake theme. Most anacondas don't grow half that long, and if they ate one person, they wouldn't need to eat the rest of the film crew for a few weeks.

LAKE PLACID, 1999

A 30-foot (9.1-m) man-eating crocodile terrorizes a town in Maine, U.S.A. Normally, Maine gets too cold in winter for any non-hibernating reptiles, such as crocodiles, to live and grow that large.

HARRY POTTER AND THE GOBLET OF FIRE, 2005

Nagini is evil wizard Voldemort's snake. At one point, she eats Professor Charity Burbage. Real snakes can't be ordered to eat things.

TEENAGE MUTANT NINJA TURTLES, 1990, 2014, 2016

These muscular movie reptiles are the good guys! Based on a number of 1980s comic books, these movies tell the story of four turtles who got covered in toxic waste, mutated, and learned the Japanese martial art of ninjutsu.

MYTH VS. FACT

SO NOW THAT YOU'RE AN
EXPERT ON REPTILES AND ON YOUR WAY
to becoming a herpetologist, let's check out how much you know. Can you separate the myths from the facts?

A REPTILES ARE SLIMY CREATURES.

B MANY LIZARDS ARE VENOMOUS.

C ALL REPTILES ARE MEAT-EATING PREDATORS.

D MODERN-DAY REPTILES ARE THE DESCENDANTS OF DINOSAURS.

E SOME SNAKES CAN FLY.

A. MYTH
They are scaly, yes, but not slimy. Most don't even live in water. Their scaly skin is dry, and it helps keep moisture in their bodies so they can survive in dry environments.

B. FACT
It was once believed that only a couple of lizards had venomous bites, but scientists have recently discovered that members of the iguana and monitor families are venomous too.

C. MYTH

Most reptiles do include some meat in their diets, but tortoises and iguanas are herbivores. Iguanas eat fruits, flowers, and greens. Tortoises eat a variety of plants, including grasses, fruits, and flowers.

D. MYTH

Members of the Crocodylia order are dinosaurs' closest reptile relatives. But scientists overwhelmingly believe that birds are the direct descendants of dinosaurs.

DON'T SUCK THE VENOM OUT!

Many old Western, or cowboy, movies show characters getting bitten by snakes and having the venom sucked out as a way to save them from certain death. In the real world, this is a big snakebite no-no. If someone is bitten by a potentially venomous snake, take these actions instead:

1. **SEEK MEDICAL ATTENTION, EVEN IF THERE ARE NO IMMEDIATE SYMPTOMS.**

2. **MAKE A MENTAL NOTE OF THE COLOR AND SHAPE OF THE SNAKE—KNOWING THE TYPE OF SNAKE INVOLVED WILL HELP WITH TREATMENT.**

3. **CALM THE PERSON WHO WAS BITTEN AND KEEP THE WOUND BELOW HEART LEVEL. THESE ACTIONS WILL HELP SLOW THE SPREAD OF THE VENOM.**

4. **IF YOU HAVE TO WAIT FOR AN AMBULANCE, CLEAN AND COVER THE BITE WOUND.**

E. FACT ... ISH

"Flying" is the term used by scientists to describe how the paradise tree snake moves from tree to tree in its jungle habitat. It can flatten and undulate its body to glide up to 328 feet (100 m).

REPTILE RAP: 200 OF THE MORE THAN 600 VENOMOUS SNAKE SPECIES ARE DEADLY TO HUMANS.

WHICH REPTILE ARE YOU?

REPTILES HAVE SOME PRETTY
AWESOME SKILLS, HABITS, AND TRAITS. WE
often describe them as having human qualities. But what if we
described ourselves using reptile qualities? Which kind of reptile
do you think you would be?

WHO'S YOUR REPTILE DOUBLE?

1 **When someone wants to pick a fight or threatens you, you:**
- **A.** give them a loud warning to stay out of your way.
- **B.** slap your head and walk away.
- **C.** quickly pull your head into your shirt and hope no one notices you are there.
- **D.** sport an angry blush and stare down your opponent.

2 **If given a choice, where would you prefer to live?**
- **A.** in a desert, preferably a warm one
- **B.** in a swamp, where it is warm and humid
- **C.** near the water, preferably a lake or stream
- **D.** in a leafy forest tree house

3 **You prefer to wear:**
- **A.** an outfit you can "shed."
- **B.** studded jackets, which are all the rage this season.
- **C.** a raincoat or parka—you prefer a protective shell.
- **D.** something different and colorful that you can change with your mood.

4 **What sounds like an excellent meal to you?**
- **A.** a large one—you don't like to snack
- **B.** You take your meals by the shore, so catfish sounds great.
- **C.** a bit of salad, some fish, or snails
- **D.** small protein snacks, eaten picnic style

REPTILE RAP: LIZARD SPECIES (ABOUT 6,000) OUTNUMBER ALL MAMMAL SPECIES (ABOUT 5,400).

IF YOU SCORED MOSTLY A:
You're like the elegant rattlesnake. You prefer to keep to yourself, but if someone bothers you, you will let them know it. You prefer things hot and aren't afraid to shed your skin to make yourself anew.

IF YOU SCORED MOSTLY C:
Like a majestic turtle, you prefer to avoid conflict rather than approach it headlong. You know your mind and where you are comfortable. And you always carry a little bit of home with you wherever you go.

IF YOU SCORED MOSTLY B:
The demonstrative alligator is your animal twin. You are quiet but also flashy, and you love the water. You'll warn those who provoke you, but hardly anyone will dare.

IF YOU SCORED MOSTLY D:
Well hello, you! Your changeable nature makes you akin to a chameleon. When someone ticks you off, you go red in the face. You are happiest just hanging out, and you aren't afraid to go out on a limb.

PHOTO FINISH

BEHIND THE SHOT WITH BRADY BARR

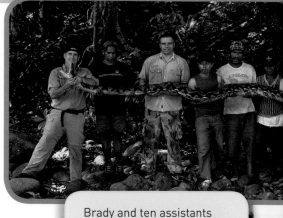

A LOT OF MY RESEARCH HAS FOCUSED ON WHAT CROCODILIANS EAT. THESE ARE CALLED DIET STUDIES,

and they help us understand what is important to a croc in the wild. You can't just protect endangered crocs in the wild to help save them. You also have to protect what is important to the animal, such as its food source. So you might ask, how in the world do you find out what is in a croc's stomach? As crocs have the most powerful jaws on the planet, the answer is: very carefully.

Croc research is dangerous work. After I catch a live croc, I must tie up its legs and snapping jaws. I place a piece of pipe in its mouth, then tape the mouth shut around it. With the croc safely tied up, now comes the fun part. I give the croc a big drink of water, then give its belly a series of big squeezes, just like you might give the Heimlich maneuver to a choking person. In fact, among croc specialists, this technique is called "the hose Heimlich technique." It is a safe way to empty the stomach without hurting the croc. With a big croc, this technique is definitely a two-person operation. Anything that is in the stomach comes right up, and I catch it in a big plastic tub. Boy, does it smell bad, but it is super cool to see what the animal has been eating. You might think that big old crocs would only be eating large prey, such as deer and other mammals, but that isn't always true. They eat a lot of small things as well, including fish, insects, and even snails. Their stomachs also include stuff other than food. It is not unusual to find sticks and stones and even human-made items in a croc's stomach.

The strangest thing I ever saw come out of a croc or gator stomach was an otter, but not the kind of otter you would expect. I was flushing the stomach of a large alligator in the Florida Everglades one night, when out pops a ball of fur from the gator's mouth and into my tub. That's not unusual, but this ball of fur blinked a couple of times, sneezed, and shook its head. It then jumped out of the tub, over the side of the boat, and swam away. It was alive! You see, crocodilians do not chew their food—they swallow it whole. Or, if the prey is particularly large, they tear it into pieces that they can swallow. The gator must have swallowed the otter whole just before I captured it. That otter was the luckiest animal on the planet that night. If I hadn't come along and flushed it from the alligator's stomach, that would have been the end for the otter. And to think I didn't even get a thank-you!

Brady and ten assistants hold a reticulated python. Reticulated pythons are nonvenomous constrictors that can grow to a whopping 22 feet (7 m). They are the world's longest snakes and longest reptiles.

Brady poses with a crocodile whose snout is kept temporarily shut for safety with duct tape, wire, and bungee cords. He carries some of the tools of his trade in his pocket, including pliers and wire cutters.

AFTERWORD

THE MOST FRIGHTENING FACT
ABOUT REPTILES ISN'T THEIR DEADLY VENOM

or their bone-crushing jaws. It's the fact that almost one-third of them are considered threatened with extinction. Nearly 100 reptile species are critically endangered. That is a lot of amazing animals that may be missing from our world someday soon.

In some cases, a limited habitat is partially to blame, such as with Komodo dragons. They live on only a few islands in Indonesia, and a natural disaster in the area could devastate their population. For other animals, an overly specialized diet can cause problems if they run out of the one food they prefer to eat. In most cases, human development, such as filling in swamplands where alligators hunt and building resorts on beaches where sea turtles nest, is the biggest reason some reptile species are in danger. Hunting also causes problems. Many cultures hunt and eat turtles, and they view turtles, and their eggs, as delicacies. Some people hunt crocs merely for sport or for their skins, which can be made into footwear, purses, and belts.

Nature has a delicate balance. If something happens to one animal, it may cause problems for other creatures, and even people. So while hunting for food and some development are necessary, we need to take care of our scaled friends. Lizards and snakes help keep pest populations down by eating insects and gulping down mice. Predators, such as alligators and crocodiles, help signal the health of their habitats. If there are plenty of top predators, that means there are also a healthy number of prey animals to feed them. While reptiles are amazing and cool creatures to look at, watch, and study, they are also important to a healthy and diverse planet.

Crocodiles are fearsome and well armored, but they are also threatened by loss of habitat and hunting. They are an endangered species. Many crocodiles are also in danger when they venture too close to roads in populated areas.

Komodo dragons have a limited range in the wild. This makes them easier to illegally hunt. They are considered a vulnerable species. Only about 4,000 to 5,000 Komodo dragons exist in the wild.

Leopard geckos have movable eyelids, which makes them different from most geckos. They love to eat grasshoppers, worms, cockroaches, and crickets.

AN INTERACTIVE GLOSSARY

REPTILE WORDS

The mossy gecko lives in the wild only on the Pacific islands of New Caledonia.

DO YOU HAVE THE HERPETOLOGIST LINGO DOWN?

Before you start handling snakes and lizards, review the words below. Afterward, check them out in action on the pages listed. The answers are featured at the bottom of this page.

1. Camouflage

The hiding or disguising of an animal in a way that makes it blend in with its surroundings
(PAGES 18, 19, 24, 26)

Which is not a type of camouflage?

a. scales that stand out in a habitat

b. coloring similar to one's surroundings

c. moving in jerky motions to look like a tree branch in the wind

d. looking like a log floating in the water

2. Carnivore

An animal that eats only meat
(PAGES 10, 25)

Which two animals are carnivores?

a. green iguana

b. painted turtle

c. Komodo dragon

d. green anaconda

3. Crocodylia

An order of large reptiles with powerful jaws that live both on land and in water
(PAGES 11, 14, 15, 37, 50, 51)

Which is not a crocodilian?

a. gharial

b. caiman

c. tuatara

d. alligator

4. Ectotherm

An animal that uses its surroundings to regulate its body temperature
(PAGES 10, 11, 19, 28, 35)

How does an ectothermic animal warm itself?

a. by being active at night

b. by swimming in water

c. by sunning itself on a rock

d. by crawling into a cave

5. Herbivore

An animal that eats only plants
(PAGES 10, 25, 50, 51)

Which animal is a herbivore?

a. desert tortoise

b. saltwater crocodile

c. boa constrictor

d. Gila monster

6. Omnivore

An animal that eats meat and plants
(PAGE 10)

Which animal is an omnivore?

a. green iguana

b. yellow-blotched map turtle

c. Komodo dragon

d. green anaconda

7. Oviparous

Producing and laying eggs from which young hatch
(PAGE 23)

Which reptile is oviparous?

a. short-horned lizard

b. alligator

c. salamander

d. chameleon

8. Ovoviviparous

Producing eggs that develop inside the mother's body. When the eggs hatch, she gives birth to live young.
(PAGE 23)

Which animal is ovoviviparous?

a. short-horned lizard

b. alligator

c. green anaconda

d. dwarf tree gecko

9. Parthenogenesis

A form of reproduction in a species of animals that are all female. Their eggs do not need to be fertilized by a male.
(PAGE 22)

Which animal can reproduce through parthenogenesis?

a. skink

b. alligator snapping turtle

c. Gaboon viper

d. dwarf tree gecko

10. Prehistoric

Describing something that is ancient or from a very long time ago, such as dinosaurs
(PAGES 7, 14, 32, 34, 36, 37, 38)

Which two of these are prehistoric animals?

a. *Spinosaurus*

b. caiman

c. gecko

d. pterosaur

11. Rhynchocephalia

An order of reptiles of which there are only two living species of tuataras
(PAGE 11)

Tuataras are rhynchocephalia species that live in the wild only in what country?

a. Australia

b. Brazil

c. New Zealand

d. China

12. Viviparous

Giving birth to live young
(PAGE 23)

Which animal is viviparous?

a. hawksbill turtle

b. nocturnal gecko

c. tussock skink

d. whiptail lizard

ANSWERS: 1. a; **2.** c and d; **3.** c; **4.** c; **5.** a; **6.** b; **7.** b; **8.** a; **9.** d; **10.** a and d; **11.** c; **12.** c

FIND OUT MORE

Reach out for more reptile information with these resources.

DOCUMENTARIES

Kids: Ask your parents for permission to watch.

Supersize Crocs
PBS Nature, 2007

The Dragon Chronicles
PBS Nature, 2009

Invasion of the Giant Pythons
PBS Nature, 2010

Black Mamba
PBS Nature, 2009

Life: Reptiles and Amphibians
BBC Earth, 2009

World's Deadliest Snakes
Nat Geo WILD, 2005

PLACES TO VISIT

Australian Reptile Park
Somersby, New South Wales

Haus der Natur—Reptile Zoo
Salzburg, Austria

Reptile Gardens
Rapid City, SD, U.S.A.

The Reptile Zoo
Fountain Valley, CA, U.S.A.

BOOKS

Firefly Encyclopedia of Reptiles and Amphibians
Chris Mattison (Ed.)
Firefly Books, 2015

Ultimate Reptileopedia: The Most Complete Reptile Reference Ever
Christina Wilsdon
National Geographic Children's Books, 2015

WEBSITES

Kids: Ask your parents for permission to search online.

endangeredspeciesinternational.org
This website features updates on conservation projects and endangered species, including reptiles.

animals.nationalgeographic.com/animals/reptiles
Articles, videos, and photo galleries on many reptile species are featured on this website.

**Editorial, Design, and Production by
Plan B Book Packagers**

Captions

Cover: A mountain sipo snake's brilliant green coloring reflects
its habitat in Ecuador's Mindo Cloud Forest.

Page 1: When threatened, the Australian frilled lizard opens its
mouth, hisses, and unfurls the skin flap around its head. The
frilled flap makes it appear bigger to scare off predators.

Pages 2–3: One of the largest gecko lizards, tokay geckos can
grow to about 14 inches (35 cm) in length.

Since 1888, the National Geographic Society has funded
more than 12,000 research, exploration, and preservation
projects around the world. The Society receives funds from
National Geographic Partners LLC, funded in part by your
purchase. A portion of the proceeds from this book supports
this vital work. To learn more, visit www.natgeo.com/info.

For more information, visit www.nationalgeographic.com,
call 1-800-647-5463, or write to the following address:
National Geographic Partners
1145 17th Street N.W.
Washington, D.C. 20036-4688 U.S.A.

Visit us online at nationalgeographic.com/books

For librarians and teachers: ngchildrensbooks.org

More for kids from National Geographic: kids.nationalgeo-
graphic.com

For information about special discounts for bulk purchases,
please contact National Geographic Books Special Sales:
ngspecsales@ngs.org

For rights or permissions inquiries, please contact National
Geographic Books Subsidiary Rights: ngbookrights@ngs.org

NATIONAL GEOGRAPHIC and Yellow Border Design are
trademarks of the National Geographic Society, used
under license.

Paperback ISBN: 978-1-4263-2526-7
Reinforced library binding ISBN: 978-1-4263-2527-4

Printed in Hong Kong
16/THK/1